102 DISTRACTIO
For Self-harm and o
strug

"Distraction"
noun

"A thing that prevents someone from concentrating on something else."
Dictionary definition on Google

This book is dedicated to the following people who have made a significant difference in my life, especially since my relapse in late 2017. I can't thank you enough for the support and encouragement you have given me.

Carla
Mum
Nigel
Dad
Mary
Nan
Lewis
Andrew
Ricky
Chris
Jolijn
David
Neil

Patricia

Without you I wouldn't have been able to keep fighting.

102 DISTRACTION TECHNIQUES
For Self-harm and other Mental Health struggles

Introduction

Mental illness is difficult to deal with, there's no denying that. Whether you're dealing with depression, having anxiety attacks or succumbing to self-harm we all need as much mental ammunition as we can get hold of. 102 Distraction Techniques is pretty much what it says it is. I, Scott, have been trying to cope with emotionally unstable personality disorder, depression, anxiety and self-harm on and off since I was 15. I'm always look for distractions to help me curb my destructive urges and help me stay positive when my mind starts playing up.

The distractions laid out in this book are ones that I have engaged in, except where stated, and they work for me. But as the mind and mental illness are so complex no distraction works for everyone, nor does it work every time. What is important is that you try different techniques until you have a range of distractions that work for you, at least most of the time. I have also shared some techniques that work for other people, I have stated which ones are from other people towards the end of this book.

Some of these distractions are pro-active, meaning that they can be practised any time to help strengthen your mind and well-being, and, some of these distractions are reactive meaning that they should be applied when you feel like your mental illness is taking over. This could be when you have self-harm urges, panic attacks, depressive episodes, manic episodes, etc. As I said before, they will not always work but through practising them, alone or with a trusted person, you can improve your chances of staying in control and staying safe. I hope these really help you.

All of the distractions laid out in this book are very simple and relatively easy to apply. I have written a simple paragraph that accompanies each distraction describing what they are and why they're beneficial to you. Please remember that none of these distractions will solve your problems but they will help you gain more control, that's the aim here.

Finally, if you know someone who is struggling with their mental health then this book gives you a list of things that you can suggest to them. Everyone who struggles needs a little encouragement so with this book you have plenty of techniques that you can suggest and re-enforce.

102 DISTRACTION TECHNIQUES
For Self-harm and other Mental Health struggles

1. Talk to someone who you trust or know well

This is without a doubt the most important alternative to suffering and struggling. I'm sure you've been told to open up about your struggles before? Talk to someone close to you who can support you through the tough times and encourage you to do things that are going to benefit your mental health and well-being. Talking about whatever is going on in your mind helps alleviate tension, stress, numbness, etc. This is because thoughts need expression and whilst they're all bottled up in your head they are causing unpleasant sensations and will eventually explode and cause harm. A problem shared is a problem halved. Sharing your thoughts is the quickest way to start feeling more relaxed. Get talking, not only to get the mess in your head out, but to let people know you need support.

2. Talk to a doctor, therapist or mental health professional

If you're battling mental health problems it's a no-brainer that you need to seek professional guidance. You can visit your doctor, a therapist or any qualified professionals in the field of mental health. Whist all these distraction techniques laid out in this book can help out in the time of need, as well as being ongoing self-care techniques, you will need ongoing support until to you reach the point that you feel you can handle and manage your symptoms. Plenty of mental disorders can't be "overcome" and you will need to learn how to manage them. The qualified professionals will help you do just that. Depending on where you live there are plenty of free services available, especially in the UK (where I'm from), that you can access. The best place to start looking is the internet, obviously. I highly suggest you apply this and the previous distraction technique as often as you can as they will be your strongest methods for achieving stability and self-control.

For those of you in school you should have a counsellor or welfare office that you can talk to.

3. Talk to someone over a support phone line

As uncomfortable as it may seem talking to a stranger over a support phone line, such as Samaritans, talking to a stranger may be the thing you need to get advice or let off some steam. Like talking to a doctor or a therapist there's no emotional connection between you and the person at the other end of the phone line. Having that emotional distance can make it a lot easier to share your feelings with another person. What you say will not affect how the other person treats you, you can speak freely and they will only do their best to be supportive. Sometimes they're just there to listen and having such a resource can make a difference to how you're feeling, especially if you feel alone. The best thing is that most of these support lines are free to call.

4. Play with a fidget or stress toy

I have an inventory of these toys and at least one stays with me at all time. Like talking they help express the tension or urges that I'm experiencing by giving my hands something to do. The movement of my hands and fingers is a way of my body talking instead of actual words having to leave my mind. Sometimes I play with them for a few minutes but sometimes I play with them for an hour or so. Stress balls and squishes are great for anger and the toys that move, such as fidget spinners or tangles, are great for coping with anxiety. Take one wherever you go and you'll always have a distraction technique available. Every time you put your hand into your pocket you'll have a physical reminder that it's there in an emergency.

5. Listen to music

Music comes in many forms and there are millions of songs for you to listen to. There's a song for every occasion, I'm sure you've spent time putting many playlists together to suit the mood that you're in. I'm no different. I don't want to keep reminding you of the fact that thoughts (accompanied by their attached emotion) need to be expressed but I want to stress it's importance. Listening to a song can help you express the emotion you're feeling. Maybe it's the sound of the instruments that help motivate you. Maybe it's the lyrics that speak to you in a way that no one else can. Or perhaps the overall vibe of the song gets you moving. Either way connecting to a particular song will help you to ride the waves of emotions and urges. Just be careful of what you listen to as some songs can trigger you and make you feel worse. If you can find a song that can help convert your negative emotions into positive ones then you're on to a winner. If you don't have a song like that right now then listen to one that pacifies the urges or tension. That's the next best thing.

6. Read a book, comic or magazine
Reading is helpful because you put all of your attention in to the words that are laid out before you. And if your attention is on the words then they're not on the things that are distressing you. Words are powerful things that can influence positive behaviours and results. I don't know about you but I like to learn and be entertained when reading, especially the former. I hope that reading this book is distracting you! If you like to read fiction then the words on a page can take you and your imagination into a place that will keep your attention distracted until your urges or negative feelings pass. If you're like me and like to read non-fiction, where you can

learn something new, you can apply what you've learnt into your life and make it a little easier and better. That's got to be worthwhile right? Books on personal development are my favourite; go and check some out as they're very inspiring and motivating. Person development books helped me gain a lot of confidence and make better use of my imagination. "How to win friends and influence people" by Dale Carnegie is a great book to start with.

7. Go for a walk, jog or run

Hopefully I don't need to explain the benefits of this one? Well as much as it should be obvious I would like to remind you anyway. First of all we all need exercise to help stay physically healthy. Secondly we need to connect with the world by going outside at some point. Finally going for a long walk, jog or run will, at some point, cause your brain to release endorphins into your body. Endorphins are what's released when you self-harm too. But using your legs is a much healthier distraction technique, or coping mechanism, than purposely injuring yourself. Not only that, you get a great opportunity to clear your head, breathe in some fresh air and soak up some sunshine, or rain if you live here in the UK. I like to use this technique the most when I feel angry as it gives me a chance to calm down. Just be careful not to overdo it please. Be sensible; keep yourself hydrated and let someone know where you're going.

8. Yoga

At the time of writing this I have only just started to try out yoga thanks to my Mum. Honestly I didn't realise how useful it can be to your mental health and well-being until I tried it out. From what I have learnt so far it helps you focus your attention to slow bodily movements and balance, as well as being a relaxation technique. After giving it a try I found it very therapeutic and relaxing, even though some of the poses were difficult to pull off. Without a doubt yoga is great for both your body and mind. I was able to keep my attention on one thing at a time, that one thing being the pose I had to emulate. If like me you're not much of a fitness person yoga is a great way to help stay calm and clear of negative emotion, especially when you have an instructor guiding you. There are many "how-to" videos online, YouTube is great, where you can learn basic yoga posses so give it a try!

9. Cardio exercises

Much like the other exercises listed in this book cardio exercises benefit your body as well as your mind. If you don't like the idea of pumping weights or leaving the house to go jogging then doing some basic cardio exercises could be for you. You can go on the internet and browse some basic exercises for you to carry out. Again, YouTube is a great place to find some workouts. The fact it involves slightly strenuous movement means that not only does it give your mind something to focus on but it also releases endorphins, which, as you probably know by now, give you a sense of satisfaction. Maybe start with some star jumps right here, right now? Like any form of exercise please make sure you stay hydrated and have something to eat some time before working out. Stretching your body is also highly recommended.

10. Lift weights, or a sensible heavy object

If you're not accustomed to weight lifting make sure you look up the best ways to lift weights so you don't injure yourself. Again, doing these kinds of exercises help release endorphins. It's also a great way to help strengthen your muscles and tone your body. I found working on my arms and upper body was a really good way of getting rid of any angry emotions I was feeling. Just make sure you give yourself time to rest in between any work out that you're doing so that you give your muscles time to repair. If you don't feel like going to the gym, or can't afford to, then use an object of a suitable weight and size for you to lift. Using a bucket with some weighty objects in it is one way. Tinned food cans can be used as smaller weights to start with. I have learnt that doing lots of reps with smaller weights is better for muscle toning and lifting heavier weights with less reps is better for muscle growth. Plenty of weight lifting exercises can be found online. Once again, YouTube is a great place to look. Please make sure you stretch your muscles before lifting weights.

11. Go for a bicycle, scooter, skateboard or rollerblade ride

These can be forms of exercises too. You're using different parts of your body to manoeuvre around and therefore... you're releasing endorphins! It's also a good way to get that much needed fresh air into your lungs. If you're into using these "rides" for extreme sports then perhaps you can go out and practice some tricks? Landing a BMX trick back in the day gave me so much satisfaction. This kind of satisfaction helps released a brain chemical called dopamine. That's another chemical that makes you feel good. If you're not into doing tricks then a nice leisurely ride will help distract you also. There's nothing like a long ride to help clear your head. I've done long bike rides to raise money for charity so if that sounds like something you want to do I suggest you do it. A long bike ride to raise money for charity will not only be a good distraction but will also give you a sense of purpose. Plan a route, get people to sponsor you, ride the route and then donate the money to a chosen charity. There are plenty of mental health charities that could do with extra money.

12. Go for a drive (as a passenger or driver)
In being a driver or passenger your attention is diverted over to the environment in which you're seeing out of the window. That in itself is a great distraction, especially if you're the driver. You've got to pay attention to the road! If you're a driver and have a car that you can drive, for example, you can go and pick up a friend to come with you for a chat

about what's bother you. I've done that plenty of times. If you can do that then you've go a really strong distraction right there. Your focus will be on the road ahead, instead of solely the thing on your mind, and you will be able to talk about your struggles too. If you fancy a bit of silence to clear your head then you can always go on your own. If you're not able to drive then perhaps a friend, parent, etc. can take you out for a drive? It gives you another opportunity to talk and stare out the window, which will help calm you down. Just be careful if you're going to drive though. If you feel really angry, disassociated, anxious, or any intense emotion that hinders your senses then please be sensible and stay off of the road until you're at a point where it's safe to drive. Until then perhaps walking is the best option.

13. Write a letter to yourself
Writing is a great form of expression and distraction. Why do you think I like to write? Writing a letter to yourself may seem bizarre but it can have the same effect as talking to another person. You can write whatever comes to mind. Unlike talking you will be far less afraid to express what's on your mind. I have written to myself to try to motivate myself. If you could see yourself in this struggle what would a more stable version of yourself say to you? What advice would a better version of yourself say? Perhaps write that out. It has worked for me. The other form of letter I've written to myself is one that is simply all of

my negative thoughts. Converting them from thoughts and emotions on to paper (or typed on a computer) really helps you let go and makes you less tense. If you want you can scrunch up the paper and throw it away, that can be helpful. It's like you've completely banished your negative thoughts. Or, if you're like me, keep some of them to read back to yourself to see what kind of state you was in. When I do this it helps remind me that I can safely express myself and stay in control during really unpleasant episodes. We need reminders of our positive capabilities from time to time.

14. Keep a diary

Just like writing a letter, or any form of expressive writing, you can blurt out all of those thoughts and feelings onto paper rather than letting them eat you up inside. With keeping a diary you can get into the habit of doing it daily, which enables you to practice a distraction technique at least once a day. That's good for you right? You don't have to read back the entries if you don't want to but if you do then you can keep log of yourself. It can be beneficial to see what you have written, especially if you feel that you've made progress. If you don't feel that you've made progress then you might learn something about yourself that you didn't realise before. You might notice a trigger that you didn't observe before. If I didn't feel like talking to anyone when I was at my lowest I could always go to my diary and "talk to it". It's still a better option than being self-destructive, even if what you write is completely negative. Who knows, maybe you can convert those entries into a book one day?

15. Create a blog or social media account (to use like a diary)

Don't fancy hand writing and prefer to use photos and videos to illustrate what you've been up to? Then an online blog or social media account could be for you. I post mental health related content on YouTube and Instagram regularly. Not only to inspire people but as a form of expression too. I'm not the only person who does this. If you go on one of the popular social media websites or apps you will find profiles that people use a diaries or blogs to share their journeys will mental health. It can also be a great way to meet people, online I mean, who are going through similar struggles as yourself so you can help give each other support. If you already have a social media account perhaps you could create a separate one purely for discussing your journey with mental health. If you're looking for other accounts to follow be be aware that people do post things that may be triggering. Personally I'm not a fan photos or videos of self-harm being uploaded, especially without a "trigger warning", but I do agree with the freedom to express yourself. It's a tough one to discuss so just be warned that following certain accounts may have that effect on you. If it does trigger you then please do yourself a favour and do not view that content. Also be aware that, depending on your privacy settings, that loved ones and total strangers may see your posts.

16. Write a poem or story

More writing the better! As well as helping you to get all those thoughts and feelings out it gives you a chance to use the creative part of your brain as well. Creativity is a form of therapy and distraction. Thinking of how to word your story or poem keeps you focused on more than just writing words. You've really got to *think* in order for those words to make sense and have meaning. There are plenty of stories and poems available online that you can read for inspiration. Writing a story or poem doesn't have to be as personal as a diary entry or letter to yourself so you may find it easier to share with someone who can read it and be inspired or entertained. If you think the story is any good you could look at getting it published. That's something to achieve! I have read poems that people have written and posted on their social media accounts to express their struggles. I think this is a great example of self-expression that others can read and relate themselves to. People, with mental illness or not, really like to read things that are relatable.

17. Clean and organise your room

You may not know this but there's a strong unconscious influence that comes from your environment, especially ones that you spend the most time in. If you don't believe me then look up what influence your environment has on your behaviour. You will spend a lot of time in your bedroom whether you have mental health problems or not. Therefore your bedroom is a key place to influence your thoughts, emotions and behaviours. The chances are that if your room is messy and you have things scattered all over the place then your thoughts will be more scattered instead of being structured. And we both know how that can end up. In my teenage years of depression I had blood red walls. Ironically that was the bedroom where I began to self-harm a lot. Do yourself a favour and keep your room clean and organised so that when you go to your room you can feel as relaxed as possible. If your room is a mess right now then spend some time to move things around and throw rubbish away. This will also help release some of the brain chemical dopamine. You'll feel like you've achieved something and that's one of the things that releases dopamine.

18. Clean and tidy other rooms in the place that you live

OK so maybe you've cleaned your room and your mind is still playing up? Go and clean some other rooms in your place of residence. If you live with parents I'm sure they would be grateful that you've gone out of your way to tidy the place up. If you live with a partner then I'm sure they would appreciate the housework being done. You could even do some tidying up in the workplace. I didn't mention this in the previous distraction technique but another benefit of cleaning and organising is that your attention has a lot to keep up with so tidying and organising your environment can help make your mind that way also. Having your environment and your thoughts organised is far less overwhelming. Organising also gives you a good chance to throw away things that are no longer needed. Old letters, nearly empty shampoo bottles, toilet roll centres, sweet wrappers, old magazines and anything other random crap that's not used can now be thrown away to make the rooms in your home or workplace a little less cluttered. You'll get a sense of satisfaction I'm sure. You'll feel even better if a parent, partner, friend or work colleague gives you some form of recognition for cleaning up. Recognition is important for your state of mind.

19. Wash and clean your car

If you're fortunate enough to be able to legally drive your own car then you can treat it in the same way as you do your bedroom. If you like to go for drives to clear your head then keeping the inside of your car clean will help. If I get in my car and have an empty coffee cup in the cup holder or crisp crumbs in my passenger seat it really winds me up and I don't feel like I can have a relaxed drive. Fortunately this doesn't happen very often as I like to "clean as I go". I drive my car every day and I do lots of thinking during my journeys so I need the environment that is my car to be clear. It will be of value to you do the same. Giving your car a good deep clean with some sanitiser and a hoover will make the inside feel brand new again. Oh and don't forget to throw away the crap you leave in the door pockets! You could also go one step further and wash the outside of your car. That level of cleaning will practically clean your mind of negative thoughts simultaneously.

20. Wash and clean someone else's car
Haven't got your own car to clean? Perhaps cleaning your parents, or someone else's, car may be a more viable option. I know it may seem like a typical chore but it's something to keep you distracted. Plus doing things for other people is generally rewarding, especially if you decide to do it rather than someone telling you to do it. For me the best part about doing something nice for someone I care about is the recognition and appreciation I receive. Even if I don't receive them I still feel good about myself for going out my way to give to someone. Giving through initiative is rewarding no matter who you are. There's something about the act of giving, when done in good spirit, that seems to unlock a good feeling within us. If you don't feel like doing it for free you can always charge a little cash!

21. Mow the Lawn
Does cleaning a car seem like a task you just can't seem to motivate yourself to do? That's understandable. Some distractions can be a little harder to carry out compared to others. But mowing the lawn is a very easy and a relatively short task. Just getting yourself outside is a good start. If the sun

is shinning outside then that will be very good for your mood. More importantly mowing the lawn involves a bit of movement and concentration. Movement in pushing the lawnmower about and concentration in checking that the grass is being cut properly. It requires less effort than washing a car but you can still put yourself in your parent's, partner's or friend's "good books" by doing a quick chore for them. If you own your own property then mowing your own lawn can still be a good distraction. It's like tidying your room but outside your house rather than inside. Don't underestimate how distracting and satisfying doing housework can be.

22. Look up Jokes
When I think of jokes I always think back to that scene in the British version of *The Office* when David Brent, played by Ricky Gervais, tries to give a motivational speech to an audience and suggests that practising laughter is good for you due to the endorphins your brain releases. Releasing endorphins through laughter is much safer than self-harming isn't it? Every now and then I find my self going online and looking for a new joke, usually a really bad one. The jokes I like are often considered to be "Dad Jokes" due to how bad they are. I also like weird and random jokes; what's white and can't climb trees?... A fridge! I heard that when I was eleven whist eating dinner and I laughed so hard I nearly face planted into my dinner plate. Whatever your taste is when it comes to humour there's millions of jokes to be found online or in books. If

you find some corkers you can save them to tell your friends. Making others laugh is rewarding in itself. Laughter is contagious and very powerful so get yourself on the receiving end of a great or terrible joke. I also find that jokes can turn your mood around much quicker than most other things do.

23. Ask a Friend or Family member if you can help them with anything

I've already touched upon a few things you can do for someone else as a form distraction, as well as being a useful person. The ones I mentioned before are a bit more strenuous and take longer and therefore are more distracting. If you've already tried tidying your room, cleaning one of the family cars and mowing the law and that didn't work for you, or they seemed like things you didn't feel like doing, then perhaps call up a friend or relative and ask them if you can help them with something. I can generally tell how loyal a person is by how often then offer to do things for me. I find it a lot easier to be get along with someone who gives unto me. Not because I like having things done for me but because they *want* to do things for me as that what true friends, or family, do. I'm fortunate to have the friends and family that I have but if I didn't do things for them from time to time I'm sure they would be fed up with me being so selfish. As mentioned in previous techniques giving make you feel good. So go out your way to help a friend or relative by asking them if you can help out somehow. I hope it goes without saying that this should be applied regularly and not just to distract yourself. You can apply this same technique for anyone, not just friends and family. People like your boss, work colleagues and even strangers will be pleasantly surprised when you go out of your way to do something for them, not matter how small. Trust me when I say, "You can only get when you give first".

24. Pray – to whoever or whatever you want

If you follow a religion or do not you can pray. You don't need to be religious. I'm not a man of religion but I do live by a philosophy which has many rules similar to that of religions. For example I live by the golden rule; "Treat others how you wish to be treated". It's a no brainer for me. I do pray though, to the Universe. In praying I get a lot of peace and my mind is often very calm for doing so. Praying is very similar to meditation in some ways. Like meditation you block out your external world by focusing on your internal world. You can pray silently in your mind or you can speak out loud whilst praying. I prefer to speak out whilst praying as my voice stays synchronised with my mind and there's a good flow that allows me to stay focused. Where as in praying silently my mind can often wander, which defeats the object of being able to focus. But what do I pray about? Mostly I use it to express gratitude for the things I have and sometimes, when I'm stuck in life, I ask for guidance. I will literally ask the Universe "What do I need to do?" I will keep asking until an answer is presented in my mind. I always feel at peace with myself and my world after praying, the feeling my not last a life time but it is enough to distract me temporarily from being self-destructive. If you've never prayed before start by expressing gratitude for anything or anyone good in your life. The expression of gratitude is often overlooked by many but when you practice this regularly you will realise that you can't feel low when you *sincerely* express gratitude for something.

25. Watch a Documentary

Unlike most brainless television shows or online videos watching a documentary gives you the opportunity to learn something interesting, which you can share with your peers. Documentaries are generally longer than the average television show or online video so your mind will be occupied with eating up information. That can be enough to distract you for an hour or so at least. That's plenty of time to let the storm pass. There's a documentary out there for everyone. Maybe nature and history interests you? Maybe you find crime to be a thrilling theme? Or perhaps something around science and technology? I quite like a good conspiracy documentary myself. Anything that is thought provoking will obviously get you questioning your beliefs and that's something you can put your mind to rather than self-destructive thoughts. You may even find yourself binge watching a string of different documentaries.

26. Watch a funny TV Show or Movie

I've already covered why laughter is a good idea; to get those endorphins released! Finding jokes online can be humorous but I think comedy shows and movies are even better. There's about one hundred years worth of comedy material in the form of movies and television shows out there which you can access through online streaming, DVDs, etc. I'm sure you have a handful of shows and movies that make you laugh till your sides split. Go and put one on. It might be a good idea to go and find some new ones to watch. Look online or ask someone to recommend one that you've not seen before. I myself am a fan of the older comedies such as Monty Python, The Naked Gun, Seinfeld and anything by the two Ronnies. Everyone has a different sense of humour but there's a wide variety of gags out there to make you laugh until you can't breathe any more. Distract yourself with the gift of laughter.

27. Watch a thrilling, action packed and dramatic TV show or Movie

Not in the mood for a laugh but fancy watching something intense? A good thriller, drama or action television show or movie can get your adrenaline pumping. Fist fights, shoot outs and badass dialogue can be a great distraction, especially if you're feeling angry. If I'm feeling angry and use movies to keep my mind occupied I love watching some hero blast a load of bad guys away. Like my comedies I love the more classic action movies, especially if they have a Sci-fi theme. Terminator 2 is one of my personal favourites. If you want to discover some great new or old action packed movies go and visit the website, or app, IMDb and look at their top 250 movies of all time. I'm still trying to work my way through the list. Also you don't have to watch these movies or television shows on your own; invite someone over to join you. That will not only distract you but the company can keep you safe and spending time with people you love will help release another brain chemical called oxytocin. Oh and if you want a recommendation for dramatic television shows I recommend Breaking Bad, Game of Thrones, Dexter and Prison Break. Binge watching shows might not be productive but it's definitely a distraction that will keep you safe.

28. Binge watch YouTube videos

This is one of my most used distractions for sure. YouTube is very accessible these days so you can have a world of videos at your fingertips. You probably have a phone that can play YouTube videos, if not a tablet, computer or smart TV is also an option. Regardless of how you access YouTube there are billions of videos you can watch. I've distracted myself from self-harm many times thanks to YouTube. There's a video for just about anything you can think of. Videos that generally work for me are Top 10 videos. I know that sounds dull but with Top10 videos I'm usually entertained and I discover something new. Discovering something can be both interesting and educational. If Top 10s don't do it for you then I'm sure you can watching something funny like compilation videos of cats being silly. Put on some YouTube videos and before you know it hours would have passed and by then you should have passed through that intense wave of negative emotion. You can always watch my YouTube channel at youtube.com/scottshrubsole (Don't forget to subscribe!)

29. Watch TED Talks and other inspiring speeches

Now, being entertained is one thing, learning something is another but in my opinion being motivated and inspired by a video is even more beneficial to your state of mind. If you can distract yourself by converting your negative thoughts and feelings into motivation and inspiration then you're getting closer to being in more control over yourself. Distracting yourself enough to be safe is good but no where near as good as actually using that distraction to convert your energy from negative to positive, and, when I say positive I mean *really* positive. Even if I'm not feeling negative I get a lot out of watching public speakers share ideas and words of wisdom. TED is a great company that organises events where inspirational people deliver speeches. You can watch TED videos online on their website and on YouTube. There are different categories for all the types of talks they have so you'll find something that will inspire you. "Start with why – how great leaders inspire action" by Simon Sinek is by far the most inspirational speech I have ever seen. I watch it often, not even as a distraction technique any more. There are other organisations other than TED that host great speakers but TED is the most superior in my opinion. Go through TED's website or search "motivational speech" on YouTube and you'll find speakers that will inspire you and you'll want to absorb all of their words. Watching these kinds of speeches are without a doubt my most favourite distraction that I can do on my own. You never know what kind of positive thoughts and behaviour can be inspired through a good speech.

30. Look up motivational quotes

Unfortunately some of the most inspirational people that ever lived were born and passed away long before the internet and YouTube was available. However their words were immortalised in books, which would then be transferred to the internet in the form of motivational quote websites. Just look up "motivational quotes" and you'll find millions of quotes from some seriously influential and inspirational people over the last few thousand years. Reading through different quotes will not only keep your mind occupied but they have the ability to make you think differently in a really positive way. Like the motivational speeches mentioned in the previous technique the quotes can help you convert your thoughts and feeling from negative to positive. My personal favourite quote is by Napoleon Hill; "Whatever the mind can conceive and believe it can achieve". Some quotes will impact you so much that they often become rules to live by and from time to time to will silently repeat themselves in your mind. An example of this is when someone frustrates me at work the quote "Hate the sin, not the sinner" pops into my mind. Just remembering that quote helps me to stay calm.

31. Put motivational quotes up in your bedroom and/or work space

Looking up motivation quotes to feel inspired is one thing, but having them visibly placed in areas that you spend plenty of time in is even better. Why? Because seeing them will help re-enforce a more positive mindset. Seeing and reading them over and over again will help the quotes stick in your mind. That's how they will be more effective in influencing your behaviour. You probably spend a considerable amount of time in your room or work space so having motivational quotes up on the walls of these places will be a clear reminder of them. Even a glance at them, instead of taking the time to slowly read them, can be enough of a prompt to stay motivated and distract you from thinking negatively. When I wake up in my bedroom I'm faced with a large black frame that bares the words "Quitters never win and winners never quit". For me this is a strong distraction from having suicidal thoughts. It helps me push myself to keep going until I succeed instead of giving up on myself. I strongly urge you to adopt a similar practice. Find some quotes that have a really thought provoking and inspirational impact on you, then either write them or print them out onto paper and then place them where you will often look. The ceiling above your bed is a good idea. So is placing them on the back of your bedroom door. Think, where do you spend a lot of time? Sometimes these quotes can have more of a positive impact on your mind than actual people trying to give you advice.

32. Put up pictures of people who inspire you in your bedroom and/or work space

Much like the motivational quotes being up on your walls, people that inspire you can also prompt you into thinking and behaving more positively. As a teenager you may prefer to cover your walls with pictures of your favourite movie star or rock band, which is fine, but perhaps add a picture of someone who helped improve mankind to your walls. I have a photo frame that contains eight people whom I find highly influential and successful. They're influential because they overcame the odds and have given something back to the world to make the lives of others better in some way. They also have personality traits and philosophies that I wish to adopt. Like the motivational quotes being on display, looking at these people, even at a glance, I feel motivated and inspired to better myself and be as positive as I can be. I think of their achievements and the tough start they had and I then think "If they can do it then so can I". Remember that the more you positivise your environment the easier it will be to feel positive. Your environment will always influence you, even without you realising it's happening.

33. Draw something
Like I've said before, thoughts and feelings need to seek expression and what better and safer way to express than through the medium of drawing. Even if you don't think you're good at drawing you can still give it a good go. You don't need to be good at drawing at all to express yourself so don't give up before you try it. Go and grab a pencil, or pen, and some paper then just let your energy and imagination flow. You could just do some scribbles or you could create something more refined, it really doesn't matter. What's important is that you put a pen or pencil to paper and let your unpleasant thoughts and feelings come out so they won't do any harm. During my teenage years, when I understood mental illness far less, I would often sit in my room and draw sad pictures with a black ball point pen and write words around them. At the time my parents thought this was "sadistic" but it made sense to me. If I didn't feel like talking to anyone I would talk to the paper with my pen instead. I wish I kept all the pictures I drew so I could remind myself how far I've come. If you decide to use this technique it might be a good idea to put the images away so one day when you're organising all your belongings you'll stumble upon these and you can remind yourself of the progress you've made. Who knows, if you're proud

of the drawing you do you could always sell them online.

34. Paint something

I mean this in the artistic sense and not the decorating sense. Though I'm confident that decorating some walls with paint would actually be an effective technique. The distraction of painting has similar effects to the distraction of drawing but I find painting to be a more relaxing form of expression. I suppose that's because I find it easier to splash some colours together to make an abstract or expressionism piece. Painting has many styles and, again, you don't need to be good at it. Just simply dipping a brush into some paint and smearing it across a canvas can be a good enough distraction to feel less tense. When I was more artistic I had a thing for painting my hands either red, grey or black then using them to print hand shapes on canvases or paper. I don't know why but I just found it to be a good distraction. To be honest I also liked drawing hands and wrists then painting self-harm cuts across them. As morbid as that may sound it was still a distraction from doing it to myself. Art therapy is actually a relatively common form of therapy that is available thanks to health organisations. If you enjoy painting, or drawing for that matter, as a form of distraction it might be worth looking online or asking your local mental health service to see if there is a local art therapy group that you can attend. It's a chance to express yourself and meet new people.

35. Cut up paper

Ok this may seem bizarre but it can actually be quite effective. I personally think this is more suited to safely expressing any feelings of anger and frustration you may have, which is quite common if you feel like harming yourself. Instead try your best to grab a stack of paper and some scissors then start cutting them up. You may find yourself being quite aggressive with the paper but that means it's working. You can go crazy and absolutely decimate the paper or you can be creative and make patterns. If it's the Christmas season you can always make snowflakes. You may have a hell of a lot of paper trimmings on the floor after this so you can benefit from the distraction of tidying up too. If someone or something has pissed you off then you can draw it onto the paper and then cut that up. In doing this it becomes a symbol of destroying something that has hurt you without actually hurting anyone involved.

36. Create something out of materials that you have

Time for some next level creativity now. If you like being creative as a form of distraction, or just in general, then perhaps it's time to make something more three dimensional. If you have creative building toys like Lego in your possession, or the money to buy a new Lego set, then that is a great idea for distracting yourself. Building a model from instructions requires a lot of concentration, much like fine art, which means your mind is going to find it a lot easier to focus on one thing. If you're a bit of a perfectionist like me then you'll read the instructions over and over again just to make sure every piece is in its right place. You can also apply this distraction by putting together some new flat pack furniture if you have that kind of money and space. If building blocks and building furniture isn't something you can do then maybe you can gather some materials you have laying about and prepare yourself to stick random bits to each other. The end result of having a load of random bits of junk stuck together may seem a waste of time but that's not what this is about. It's about the process. The process of being creative is what's important for your mind. You don't need to make a masterpiece to distract yourself from the demons in your head. The most beneficial way of applying this distraction technique is to combine it with either one or more of the previous three techniques. Heard of a vision board? Look them up and perhaps that will inspire you as well as distract you.

37. Make a collage of photos, or anything that is associate with happy memories

You can do this just as easily with photo frames. Happy memories are important for us to hold on to as they generally remind us that life has its ups, not just downs. Nothing captures memories quite like a photograph. Time is captured within a single image for us to remember again and again. This distraction technique has not one but two benefits. The first being that you get to go through all your favourite photos and be creative by putting them together in a frame or onto a board. The second being that you can place this photo frame or collage somewhere where you'll see it often, like your bedroom wall. You may have loads of photos on your wall anyway, like the ones of inspirational people that I suggested earlier, but you can never have too many happy photos up on display. It's just going to add to your positive environment, which will help positively influence you on a subconscious level, which will then go on to affect your behaviour. The year 2018 was pretty rough for me, mostly in the first 70 percent of it, but for Christmas that year my Dad gave me a present to remind me of the good that came out of it. It was a photo frame bearing photos that captured some really happy moments of that year. Moments that I took for granted at the time due to my mental health. But looking at these photos helped remind me that 2018 wasn't as bad as I once believed it was.

38. Play video games

This is easily another one of my favourite distractions. This is due to the fact that it's very easy for a video game to hold your attention and keep you going for hours. That's more than enough time for your unpleasant urges or feelings to fade out. There are so many different video games, old and new, for you to play. If you're a serious gamer then you probably already have an inventory of games that will keep you distracted. Even if you're not a serious gamer, or don't have a console, it's relatively easy to get hold of a console and a game that can keep you interested enough to stay positively occupied, as long as you have the money to afford this form of entertainment. I have a small collection of games and consoles but each of them keep me safe. I've noticed that depending on what negative emotion I'm feeling depends on what game will keep me distracted. When I feel anxious or depressed I tend towards playing Pokemon Go on my phone whilst going out for a walk. If I feel angry or frustrated I will play something like Call of Duty, Doom or Resident Evil. Something with guns and violence basically. Pokemon Go and other hand held Pokemon games are bright in colour, easy to play and have a progressive structure about them. They're simple and rewarding so I find it easy to play whilst depressed or anxious. Shooting based games really do it for me when I'm angry or frustrated as I can blast enemies away without doing any actual harm. I can let anger out safely this way. You may find yourself playing similar games but at the same time you may prefer a different kind of RPG, FPS or even a different genre altogether. But as I said, there's a game out there to keep anyone distracted. If you can play online with your friends and communicate through a headset then you've got an additional distraction to utilise. Some people slate video games for being an unhealthy addiction but it's definitely better than hurting yourself.

39. Get a haircut

I feel like a million pounds when I get a haircut, especially if it's been over a month. A cut or change in style can give you a nice confidence boost, as well as an opportunity to natter to the person cutting your hair. As much as I agree with the inside of a person being the most important, having a little improvement to your looks, such as a fresh trim, can also make you feel better on the inside. I used to have a typical emo fringe when I was seventeen, then I went for a more long haired look but when I got a promotion to assistant manager in this restaurant I worked at I got it cut a lot shorter. I felt like this haircut represented me as I wanted people to see me; confident and successful. It may seem a little vain but a little vanity can work wonders for your emotions, which in turn will help you think more positively instead of negatively. Plus, isn't it nice when people notice and compliment you on your new haircut?

40. Have a makeover

This one isn't just for girls you know! I used to wear eyeliner as a teenager. I even got dressed up as a girl and had full make over once or twice, I'm not ashamed to admit that! Regardless of your gender why don't you look online at some different make-up styles or trends and give one of them a go? Even better would be to get a friend round to your place, who is experienced in the application of make-up, and get them to do it for you. That's another opportunity to have someone to talk to and be distracted. If you can combine this with the previous distraction then you're on to a winner. I don't personally wear make-up any more but my partner, who also has emotionally unstable personality disorder, says that it does wonders for her motivation and confidence, as well as being a distraction through taking time to apply it. Again if you feel that you look good on the outside it will help influence you feeling good on the inside. Playing around with different styles is both fun and creative. Don't worry about making it look good if you're not in the mood for perfection, just go crazy!

41. Try on new clothes

OK this one may seem like another thing for the girls to do but anyone can give this a try. Growing up as a teenager with mental illness I was pretty stuck with the emo look for a few years but towards my early adult years, and trying to better myself, I started to change my choice of clothes too. Like having a hair cut or makeover, changing your style can be a good idea to help give yourself a confidence boost, as well as being a bit of a distraction and coming out of your fashion comfort zone. Even if you have no money right now why don't you and a friend or relative go to one of your favourite clothing shops and try on some clothes that you like the look of? You can always keep note of what you like and come back another time when you have money. After I relapsed

I found myself doing lots of window shopping looking at clothes that were a bit different to the usual style I would wear, mostly smart casual clothes. As well as keeping myself busy with browsing I would eventually buy these clothes and wear them out and about. This gave me a little boost in how I perceived myself as it was a reminder that I could look attractive. Feeling attractive does help your confidence, especially if you're trying to look for someone to have a relationship with. Trying on new clothes, or updating your wardrobe may not be the best "reactive distraction" but it definitely helps how you feel about yourself in your day to day life. Combine a new outfit with a makeover and/or haircut and that will help your brain release serotonin, another one of the four happy brain chemicals. I love putting on skinny tartan trousers, a smart top and a trendy jacket. I feel good about myself and that helps defend me against self-doubting thoughts. I know this seems superficial and vain but there's no harm in that if it helps your state of mind.

42. Dress smarter more often

Again this distraction is more of a proactive distraction than a reactive distraction, and this technique co-insides with the previous technique. But I want to make this one a distraction technique of its own because of the impact it has had on me. As mentioned in earlier in this book, your environment plays a big part in influencing your thoughts, feelings and behaviours. Technically speaking your environment is anything outside of yourself, including your clothes. Your outfit isn't just a reflection of how you're feeling, it also influences that feeling right back to you. In my teen years I always dressed in black because I generally felt miserable, but looking back I know it contributed even more to that feeling. Since relapsing I've tried to make more effort in my grooming and outfits. It has definitely helped my state of mind when staying in doors or going out. Rather than sitting in jogging bottoms to work on this book I prefer to get washed, trim my beard and dress accordingly. I feel ready to get things done rather than feel like a slob. If there's an opportunity for me to wear a suit, like a meeting, I jump at the chance to look my best. When I put a suit on I feel so damn successful, and not like a failure which my mind tries to tell me from time to time. Before going out, or even when staying in doors, if you can motivate yourself to do so, make the effort to look your best. You will notice that you can get more done and that your self-perception will improve. You don't have to put on your best outfit ever day, have a fresh haircut and spend hours putting make-up to make this work. Just try to make more effort with your appearance on a regular basis and you will notice a difference in your behaviour.

43. Cuddle a soft toy
At the time of writing this I'm approaching the age of twenty nine and I still have cuddly toys. This doesn't

make you a child or immature. I have a collection of soft Pokemon plushies that get a cuddle from me, especially if I'm struggling to fall asleep. Cuddling a person helps release oxytocin but if you don't have another person to hug right now then a cuddly toy is a great alternative. As weird as it may sound I talk to them when cuddling them. They may have no words to offer me in return but the fact I'm getting my thoughts and feelings out is a safer alternative to hurting myself. If you're like me and regress to a child like state from time to time cuddling a soft toy can be very comforting, so don't be ashamed to try it. It definitely helps me feel calmer. If you don't have one I suggest you buy one.

44. Cuddle your duvet

Don't have a soft toy or person to cuddle? Then perhaps your duvet cover on your bed can get some love. It really helps if you're struggling to sleep too. Most nights I sleep with my bed cover between my legs and arms as if I was spooning it. I generally get to sleep quickly through this position. Some of you may prefer to lay underneath your duvet when feeling depressed or distressed but cuddling it can help release oxytocin, which you will need to help fight off those unpleasant thoughts and feelings. If you feel like you need to cry, which is more than ok to do, then cuddling your duvet whilst crying is a safe alternative to being self-destructive. It may not completely distract you in an instant but it can definitely keep you safe enough till the storm passes.

Plus, this requires very little effort compared with the other techniques in this book.

45. Cuddle a person

When you're feeling low and your mind is going into places that it shouldn't there's nothing like cuddling someone that cares about you. From my experiences I've noticed that cuddling people I love releases way more oxytocin than wrapping my arms around my duvet or a soft toy. Whether it's my partner, my Mum, my best friend, or anyone close to me I feel safe and cared about when we put our arms around each other, which then enables my mind to start calming down. I probably don't need to go into much detail with this technique as I can guess you probably enjoy a cuddle with people that you care about but I want to emphasise its importance. In my opinion this is one of the most important ways to distract your mind from negativity. Not only does a proper cuddle release oxytocin but it helps give you the opportunity to open up to the person you're cuddling. By now you know that talking about your struggles is one of the best things you can do for your well-being right? I thought so. If you've been emotionally distant recently, or your whole life, and cuddling has been something you've not done much of then please give it a try. Cuddling is a very warming and calming experience.

46. Smile

If you have a true reason to smile then that's fantastic but I want to discuss choosing to put on a forced smile. According to psychologists forcing a fake smile can help improve your mood. I have given this a try and it does work. Not all the time of course, especially when I'm really low or angry, but if my negative mood isn't too intense it does help. When I'm at work I make a lot of effort to smile at my colleagues. Not only does it give me a little boost but as smiles are infectious it generally makes other people smile back at me. It may seem silly to force a smile upon your face, especially if strangers are looking at you, but it's worth giving a go in order to distract yourself. Sometimes I like to smile at myself in the mirror. It looks silly and I ended up laughing at myself, which is actually very good for your well-being. This one requires little effort or resources so it's worth trying before dismissing it as a waste of time.

47. Laugh

I know I've touched upon laughing in previous techniques but like the last distraction technique I want to focus on forcing yourself to laugh. You don't need a reason to laugh, you just need get yourself to laugh. I end up laughing when I go into manic episodes or when something around me happens that I find funny but when I feel stressed or low I try to laugh my way out of it. I've used this technique whilst in previous jobs as it's something I can do that doesn't stop me from working. I know that when I put on a fake laugh during negative experiences that I'm just trying to get through them without causing harm and that I'm not actually finding that particular experience funny. But it does eventually turn into that and I can see the funny side, which is totally fine. It's better to laugh than cry generally, especially if it's going to distract you enough from feeling like shit. People may think you're strange for just "randomly laughing out loud" but that doesn't matter as it's you who understands why you're doing it. Go on, bellow out a nice big chuckle!

48. Start a collection

Some people say that obsessions can be unhealthy, which I can agree with if the obsession is destructive. But if collecting things that you love, or that interests you, makes you happy then that's healthy right? If you already like to collect certain things then that's great. Make time to distract yourself by looking at your collections when you need to. If you don't collect anything at the moment then now is a good time to start. I have no idea what interests you but I'm confident you know what you could start collecting. I collect all things Pokemon; cards, video games, toys, etc. and every time I look at my collection I feel proud of myself and grateful for having earned them. I get a lot of enjoyment out of seeing my collection grow and grow and looking over it daily it helps release those much needed happy brain chemicals. I can pick up something from my Pokemon shelf, have a little play with it and my mind will focus on that instead. Think about what you like and see if you can start a collection some how. I will add at this point that you must be careful not to let yourself overspend to expand your collection. A while ago I gave my Mum my spare money as I would buy a lot of Pokemon merchandise impulsively that I realistically couldn't afford so now my collecting is a lot more reasonable, the waiting makes it more worthwhile too. It becomes something to work towards.

49. Meet with friends or family for tea, coffee or a bite to eat

I get a lot of enjoyment out of this one, especially since being a working adult that doesn't have a lot of free time. I have used this technique more as a pro-active distraction than a reactive distraction but both can be just as effective. Meeting a friend or relative at their or your place can be more beneficial than meeting them in a public cafe or restaurant because you may feel more comfortable opening up to them to talk about your struggles. I actually prefer meeting with people at one of my local coffee shops because getting out of the house and doing some walking or driving is an additional distraction to me. If you're feeling really anxious about going outside then have them pop round for a "coffee chat" instead. If I feel really anxious I don't like going out to meet people. But there's something about talking over a hot drink or food that makes everything feel a little more relaxed than if you were talking to a therapist in an office for example. I find that it helps me stay calmer which enables me to talk about my struggles more comfortably. If you don't have any money you can always ask for tap water instead. I highly suggest that you utilise this distraction on a regular basis. Any distraction technique in this book that influences a conversation must become your valuable ones.

50. Engage in your hobbies

I'm confident almost everyone reading this book will have at least one hobby they can engage in to distract themselves from negative thoughts and feelings. I myself treat my Youth Potential project more like a hobby than a job. I love working on Youth Potential and that's what makes it more of a hobby than anything else. If you're someone who goes to school or has a job then it's highly important that you have a hobby to balance yourself out with the amount of work you have to do. Too much work and not enough play is going to make it extremely difficult for you to feel good about yourself and think more positively. If you already have some hobbies such as sports, video games, reading, crafting things, etc. then turning to one of these to distract yourself is a safe and sensible option. You pick your hobbies based upon your interests and desires. The things that interest you and that you desire should be more powerful than any negative emotion or thought. This isn't always the case as depression can stop you from being interested in the things that you usually love but if you can just push yourself, or get someone else to encourage you, into engaging in your favourite hobby then that will get the ball rolling. Using your hobbies as a distraction can be difficult to start but once you get into it you may just find yourself feeling love for your hobby instead of feeling negative. But don't just turn to your hobbies in the time of need otherwise they will not distract you. Make sure you engage in them often so you can keep developing your love for them. That love is what will help distract you.

51. Start a new hobby

If you don't have a hobby I highly suggest you think about the things you enjoy and then how you can make them into a regular thing that you can engage in. If you're really stuck then use an internet search engine on your phone, tablet or computer and type in "list of hobbies". There is a vast amount of things you could give a try, and with little or no money. The best part about trying a new hobby is that you're likely to learn something new. Learning itself takes up a lot of your attention, which means it's a distraction. If you're not sure what hobby you should try then perhaps speak with someone close to you whom could suggest something to you. Better still, they may have a hobby that you can join in with. Remember that you don't need to be good at anything in particular to make it a hobby. Also bare in mind that some hobbies can turn into being money makers!

52. Eat chocolate

This may sound unusual but eating chocolate, according to scientists, helps release endorphins and is also thought to help increase your serotonin levels. This all depends on the ingredients of the chocolate but this is generally true in most cases. That doesn't always mean that it's a distraction though as eating too much will contribute to increased weight, damaging your teeth and even impairing your cognitive skills. According to the World Health Organisation twenty five grams is the recommended amount. If you're feeling low then perhaps the best thing to do is eat a standard sized chocolate bar and then carry out at least one of the other distractions listed in this book. Perhaps share a bar of chocolate with someone close to you and have a conversation about how you're feeling? Chocolate is also very good if you're feeling very anxious and shaky.

53. Volunteer for a charity

If you have plenty of free time then volunteering for a charity could be a very powerful distraction, as well as an experience to help you grow as an individual. The distraction of charity work is obviously limited to the hours in which they need you to operate for them but don't let that put you off. There are so many benefits to working for a charity, especially if you have little or no work experience. The first benefit is that it takes up your time and attention, which is a strong distraction. Secondly you will be giving your time to help benefit a charitable cause.

Giving of yourself to help an important cause should be beneficial to anyone's well-being. As I've mentioned in previous distraction techniques, giving and doing things for people, without expecting anything in return, will make you feel good about yourself, as long as you give willingfully. Finally, working for a charity looks really good on your CV. So if getting a job is on your to-do list then charity work is a great place to start if you're struggling to get a job through a lack of work experience. It proves that you're willing to work for nothing and that you're selfless. Any good employer will recognise and appreciate that kind of mentality. If you're not in work or education and struggle with your mental health I would highly recommend charity work of some kind. You need to keep yourself busy and be around people. Too much free time can be a killer as you'll be alone with any unpleasant thoughts that come your way.

54. Play sports

I'm not a very sporty person at all. In school I enjoyed sports but when depression hit me at the age of fifteen I really struggled to get myself involved in them any more. However after relapsing at the age of twenty seven I pushed myself to play some football from time to time during the summer. From the amount of movement that's going on with your body during a game of sport you will get plenty of endorphins to help you feel good. Like most distractions on this list, that require more motivation than others, you might want someone to help get you started. Once you do start playing some sports with friends or relatives you may notice how quickly your mind is distracted. Not only does the exercise help release endorphins but the competitive aspect of the sport will help release dopamine. That's two brain chemicals released from one activity! There are so many sports and even if you're not a sporty person, like me, you can give them a go just for fun. Look up what kind of sports you could try and then find someone to play with or against. Even kicking a ball up against a wall again and again can be enough to distract you.

55. Have a day out with friends or family
There are so many things you can do for a day out. All of them can be highly distracting. It's not just the event or activity that will distract you but being around your loved ones and sharing the experience with them will also distract you. As dull as it sounds I like going to a shopping centre with my Mum to go around the shops and have coffee. This distraction does generally involve spending money so bare that in mind but it will be worth it as long as you can afford it. If you can plan a day out in advance with friends or family then that gives you something to look forward to. In my teenage years of depression one of my favourite days out was for my friends and I to take a train into Camden town in London, do some shopping, grab a bite to eat and relax down by the river. Again, spending a whole day with people who care about you and going out is a strong distraction.

Although expensive going to a theme park is a really good distraction as riding on a roller coaster will get adrenaline pumping through your veins. If you want something a little more relaxed then how about going to the beach? If you're unsure of what to do just go online again and search for things to do near you. The more you do with loved ones the better you'll feel, trust me. Don't keep isolating yourself.

56. Have a night out with friends or family
Ok this may just seem like a copy of the previous distraction but going out of an evening can be more beneficial, especially if you're like me where you're more likely to feel low in the evening. Apparently it's quite common to struggle with your mental health more in the evening. I believe this is due to the fact that thinking and being active during the day uses up a lot of our energy and when we become tired it's easier for us to start descending emotionally. After a year of relapsing I got my anti-depressants changed to a slow release version because I realised that I would become easily depressed of an evening. Anyway, there are things you can do with friends or family that you're more likely to do and enjoy of an evening. This can include things like going for a drink, going to the cinema or eating at a restaurant. Of course you could do these things during the day but of an evening, when a lot of people aren't at work, you've got a better chance of being surrounded by more of your loved ones than you would if it was, for example a Monday morning. I like going out in the

evening on a weekend for a drink with my friends because I make the effort to look my best and there's usually a really good vibe for me to feed off of. I honestly believe that going out during the day is great but going out in the evening is more beneficial for me as that's when I'm more likely to dip. Perhaps the same could apply to you?

57. Take a holiday or break

Life is very demanding, especially if you work for a living. If you attend school you may not have the luxury of being able to take a holiday or break at your choosing; you will have to rely on half terms and bank holidays. But if like me you have a job then it's important to take time off on top of your usual days off. I have worked in catering, at the time of writing this book, for nearly thirteen years and it's a very demanding job. Without a holiday to look forward to I wouldn't have made it this far. Don't get me wrong I enjoy my job but sometimes I just need to get away from it to feel like I'm more than just an employee. If you're struggling with your mental health whilst at work then perhaps it's time to take sick leave in order for you regain some strength. During my relapse I ended up take five months off of work. I was lucky to be supported by my manager during this time as I definitely needed time to stabilize myself. Since relapsing I have made more effort to book extra days off where I can so I can have a better work-life balance. Make sure you get some rest during your time off. If you're highly active whilst not at work or school then it can feel like you've not had a chance to re-cooperate when you do go back.

58. Play with a pet or take them for a walk

Just like cuddling a person playing with, or stroking, a pet causes your brain to release oxytocin. If you love animals then this will probably be a popular distraction for you. Some health organisations and services offer therapies that use domesticated animals as a way of bringing comfort to the patient. This isn't just the case for patients with mental health problems either. I have seen news footage of patients, that are receiving treatment for physical conditions, in hospital been given "therapy dogs" to hold and stroke so that they feel more relaxed whilst being stuck in their hospital bed. If you don't have a pet of your own to play with then you may know someone who you can visit that owns a pet. Perhaps you could go to their home for a chat and at the same time you can stroke their dog, cat or rabbit? I feel very calm when I visit my Mum and her dog comes up to me for attention. I give him a good stroke and scratch before throwing his ball for him to fetch a few times. Being wanted by an animal feels good. I know that some people talk to their pets as a form of comfort, which sounds odd but as you get to express yourself it's still a safe alternative to hurting yourself.

59. Hold a baby

This is distraction is more suitable for people who don't have their own baby to hold. As a parent of two children I know that negative feelings can come easily, especially when you've recently had a baby, so holding your own child may not be the best distraction for you at this point. But for those who don't have a baby, meaning that you can come and go as you please, holding a baby in your arms can bring a sense of calm like nothing else. During my relapse my closest friend and his partner had a baby boy that I went to visit. When I picked him up and held him for the first time everything that was on my mind just faded away. Not only did I get an oxytocin release but my focus was on making sure that I held him correctly so that he could lay sleeping comfortably. It was a joyous occasion for me, plus his parents could take a short break whilst I held their son. As a grown up you want children to feel comfortable and protected. This helps put all of your attention on them instead of your own problems. If you know someone who has a baby this is a great opportunity for you to go and visit them. I'm sure they will appreciate your company and your help with holding the baby as they have to spend most of their time with their baby in their arms.

60. Play with a child

Much like the previous distraction this is more suitable for people who don't have their own children, don't get to see their children often or access to their own children. I myself wasn't able to see my own children during the earlier stages of my relapse, due to my behaviour, but when I eventually got to see them all my struggles disappeared, if only for a short time. There is so much joy that can come from playing fun and imaginative activities with a child. Children, especially young children, have an interesting and innocent perspective on everything so engaging in play time with them feels very safe and positive. At this time I have a seven year old brother who, like me, loves Pokemon so teaching him about Pokemon and playing the video games with him becomes very relaxing. When I play with my eldest daughter, who at this moment is five years old, we tend to play make believe games with her toys and I can't begin to tell you how funny it is. You're using up a lot of your imagination when you have to entertain and engage with a child, especially during make believe role playing games. Everything feels a lot less serious when you do this and you can get a lot out of giving a child someone friendly to play with. Have a friend or relative with a child? Go and pay them a visit and if their child wants to play with you then take that opportunity!

61. Call, message or visit a friend or relative that you've not contacted for a while

Friends and family are more vital to your well-being than almost anything else. We go through life meeting and spending time with a vast amount of people, most of which we eventually lose contact with for one reason or another. I think it's really sad that we have such wonderful moments and share so many experiences with people and then we never speak to them again. It's generally not due to the fact that we don't like them any more, the bond just fades away because we get so busy with our own lives and we just become socially lazy. But getting back in contact with that cousin you've not spoken to in years or that friend you used to have in school can bring a distracting and meaningful spark back to your life. I'm have lucky to have friends and family that I almost never get to see but still make the effort to contact me from time to time. I can tell you now that it brings me a strong sense of worth when they do. It's enough to turn my unpleasant mood around into a more positive one. I enjoy receiving a call from my Mum or one of my close friends, I'm more used to be contacted by them, but when someone like my Uncle, who lives on the other side of the planet, sends me a birthday card I feel appreciated and loved. When I message my friend Tom, who I haven't seen for years, and he texts me back to see how I'm coping I feel appreciated and loved. After my relapse I had a nightmare that one of my best friends, from my school years, took his own life. I woke up crying because of how real it felt. I hadn't spoken to him for about twelve years but I had to find out if he was ok. It took a little while to get in contact with him but when he replied to me it cleared the anxiety I had been experiencing for the previous twenty four hours. The point I'm trying to make is that if you get in contact with an old friend or relative and they reply it will work wonders for your mind and self-worth. Knowing that someone still thinks enough of you to reply to you should make you feel valued, which is a nice feeling and a distraction.

62. Retail therapy

Approach this distraction with caution. If you, like me, have impulsive spending habits then you should be careful. And if you have little or no money right now then please turn to another distraction. Anyway, *they* say money can't buy happiness and that is very true. But money does buy a distraction if done sensibly. Instead of spending money online and having to wait, because that will be a delayed distraction, why not go out with a friend or relative to your local shopping mall or city centre? Having someone there with you is a distraction in itself but you can tell them at the beginning of the outing to not let you get impulsive with your spending. If I don't have much money when my partner and I go out I tell her to stop me from being impulsive and buying lots of Pokemon cards. They're my poison I can assure you. I also let my Mum look after the majority of my money so I don't have the ability to overspend. If you want to go out and treat yourself to some nice things then maybe you should give your money to the person you're with. If you're feeling depressed it's easy to throw money at material things for a quick "buzz" and the regret it later when your mind is a lot clearer. If you let someone help control your spending you can go around the shops, try on some new clothes, check out the latest movie releases or look over some wicked pieces of tech without buying things for the sake of it. You deserve to have nice things but if you want to still be able to afford to live you need to be careful. What I like to do is look at something I like then walk away so it gives my reasoning faculties the chance to work out if I need it or want it bad enough. More often than not I don't buy that something because I know I don't need it, want it bad enough or can't realistically afford it. If you have spare money to spend then going out shopping with someone is a great distraction. Not only can you buy some nice things but it's an opportunity to talk with someone, stretch your legs and keep yourself busy. Please don't waste your money on gambling. You will never win back more than you spend.

63. Throw away crap you never use

I think we are all guilty of keeping things that no longer have any value or use. I used to struggle to get rid of things because "they might get used one day". The same can be said for things that are attached to a memory and have more of a sentimental value. If you went through all of your possessions and were honest with yourself I bet you could throw away a lot of junk. When I "deep clean" my room I always have a sack ready because I know there will be things I've kept, for whatever reason, but when I re-discover them I know they have no use to me any more. If you're going to apply the distraction of cleaning your room then it will be even more effective if you can apply this distraction at the same time. Throwing out your useless possessions is like the physical equivalent of clearing your mind; you take things you've been holding on to and get rid of them. It literally feels like that for me and I'm confident it can have the same effect on your mind. Get a few waste sacks ready and go through all your things. Be brutally honest with yourself. Will you ever go through those scraps of paper in your drawer? Will you ever read that book again? Will you wear that top ever again? This activity will keep you distracted for longer than you may think. You don't have to bin everything either. You can sell or donate some of it and let those items bring joy to someone else.

64. Ping an elastic band on your wrist

If you have ever been in therapy or have received any support from professionals then it's more than likely that you have have be told about this distraction technique. The idea of putting an elastic band on your wrist, and pinging it whenever you feel the urge to self-harm, is to replicate the feeling of cutting yourself but in a safe manner. It's as simple as that. The vigorous pinging of the elastic band will contribute towards the release of endorphins, which should help you feel a little more relaxed Keep an elastic band on you at all times and you will have access to this distraction at anytime. Please don't turn your nose up at this one just because every therapist recommends it.

65. Squeeze ice cubes

If you have access to a few ice cubes then this can be a really effective distraction. All you have to do is literally squeeze an ice cube or two in your hand with a tight and firm grip. It may sound like a waste of time but it won't be long before you realise that the ice cubes are starting to give the palm of your hand freeze-burns. For some people it's not very easy to keep the ice held so tightly in the palm of their hand and they will let go because the freezing temperature becomes too much. I personally, and I'm sure plenty of other people will be the same, have to go through a couple of ice cubes before it becomes to uncomfortable to squeeze the ice. The ice will eventually cause the palms of your hands to go numb and at this point you will have endorphins flowing through you. Although the ice does cause a little pain it's perfectly safe. Honestly I think this is one of the better distractions if your urges to hurt yourself are high as you will get some pain from it without actually causing any damage. Your pain receptors will react to the ice very quickly and your mind will focus on the uncomfortable sensation. Get yourself an ice tray to leave in your freezer so that you have access to this distraction in the time of need.

66. Eat something healthy

If you already have a healthy diet then this may not do anything for you but if you're anything like me your diet is at least half junk food. I never feel good about myself when I eat junk food, especially when I'm eating to try and comfort myself. The only exception is when I get endorphins from eating a sensible amount of chocolate. If I'm not feeling mentally great and I'm hungry I try to eat something with nutritional value. I feel proud of myself for not turning to junk food, which I know isn't any good for my body and anything that isn't good for my body is also not good for my mind either. For me I try to stay very conscious of how much sugar I intake as in the past I have over indulged. Bad diets do affect you mentally, you can look it up if you don't believe me. I'm not saying you should only eat healthy, because I don't, but it's important to balance the good grub with the bad. Your doctor is the best person to talk to for advice on healthy eating. The next time you feel low and want to eat something to comfort yourself try a piece of fruit or a chicken salad for example. I know food is a sore subject for some but a sensible diet is imperative to the ongoing maintenance of your well-being.

67. Draw lines on your body

This is a very simple distraction that I've had plenty of people suggest to me. If you have the urge to cut yourself then grab a red felt tip pen (any pen can be used but red felt tip will be most effective) and draw lines where you would want to cut yourself. The red lines are meant to look like cuts so from a visual perspective it will have a similar affect as seeing real cuts on your body. Obviously this is a safe alternative and distraction. If you don't have a red pen then just use any pen that will create visible lines on your skin. If you want you can leave the lines on your skin instead of washing them off then the affect of them may last longer because actual cuts would last a while. If you want to go one step further you could ever put plasters over them to make it feel more real in your mind, that may strengthen the effects of this distraction and alternative. Again this may seem like a waste of time but don't overlook this.

68. Do the washing up

I have put a lot of basic chores in this book as you may have noticed. As tedious as they may seem I'm a firm believer of cleaning and organising being a healthy distraction. If you live with your parents then offering to do the washing up, or loading the dishwasher at least, after a good meal can be both a distraction and a demonstration of appreciation. If you're a teenager, or child, it's easy to take your parents for granted when it comes to household chores, as they probably do most of them, so offering to washing up will be a nice surprise for them. How does this benefit you? Well, there's the fact it will keep you and your mind occupied but more importantly you should feel useful for helping your parents out. I can tell you from experience that doing a chore is less labouring when you choose to do it rather than someone telling you to do it. I can also tell you from experience that during your mental health struggles, especially as a teenager, it's easy to fall out with your parents, especially at the dinner table. This has happened to me many times I can assure you. If this has happened then it's likely you're feeling and thinking negatively somewhat. A good way to make it up to them or "calm the storm" will be to clean and wash up after dinner. They will respect you more for that than if you just went up to your room.

69. Put your favourite distractions techniques up on a wall

Visual prompts are powerful tools of influence. You're going to need plenty of visual prompts to help you cope with your mental illness until you get into the habit of being able to distract yourself more easily. Even then visual prompts are still worth having. Earlier in this book I've written about having positive quotes and inspirational people up on your wall but there's also one more thing you should seriously consider. In states of panic, anger, low mood, etc. it can be difficult to remember to use distraction techniques, until you build up the habit of using them regularly, so having a list of your favourite ones on your bedroom, or any space you spend time in, will be completely invaluable. I'm willing to bet your room is the place you try to seek out in a crisis so a list of your favourite distractions is going to get the most use there. Pick five to ten distractions, from this book or elsewhere, write them large and bold on a piece of paper then stick them on a space on your wall. Try to keep it away from other posters and shelves as best as you can because you want the list to stand out rather than blend in. The ceiling above your bed could be ideal. Just a quick glance at the list could be the difference between you defusing your intense emotions safely and doing yourself harm.

70. Look up interesting facts
Every Christmas, since 2002, I have been given the latest copy of Guinness World Records. I also watch a lot of YouTube channels that broadcast funny and interesting factual stories and events. "Be Amazed" is a great channel for this. Sometimes I even Google "Interesting Facts" to learn something new. Why do I do this? I like to be entertained and I like to learn something new. Interesting facts, to me at least, are both entertaining and educational. When something is both entertaining and educational it will hold my attention, even long after I've finished reading the article or watching the video. If it grabs my attention then it's a distraction. It's important to keep your curiosity aroused. Did you know Koalas have finger prints? Did you know movie trailers used to be shown after a movie had finished? Did you know the fear of long words is called "hippopotomonstrosesquippedaliophobia"? There's a few facts for you. Once you've looked through some genuinely interesting, or absolutely ridiculous, ones you can always share them with your friends. My Mum loves it when I tell her about the person with the worlds longest nose hair or finger nails.

71. Answer online surveys

There are companies, organisations and individuals that put surveys online to help them with something they're researching, usually a new product or service that they provide. Why not help them out by filling out a quick survey? As this involves reading it will gain your full attention. Some surveys are long, some are short, some are fun and some are very serious but it will distract you as you will have to really think about the answers you give. If you're thinking about answers then you're thinking about something other than the unpleasant things that were going through your mind. If you want more of an incentive other than a distraction then some companies will offer discounts and offers for your time. That's worth doing right? If you find that doing a few surveys is too dull you can take a short online quiz as an alternative. There are plenty of apps that offer these sorts of things. If you fancy doing some research yourself there are websites that allow you to make your own surveys for other people to take, such as Survey Monkey. Please don't use online surveys for a diagnosis of a mental illness. Only seek that sort of advice from a doctor or mental health professional.

72. Look through mental health organisation or charity websites

If you believe that knowledge is power then it's worth knowing as much as you can about your mental illness. There are *loads* of websites run by charities and organisations that specialise in mental health disorders, some general some specific. You probably knew this already but they're still worth looking over from time to time. If mental illness is something that you've recently started to struggle with then reading the content on these websites is the first thing you should do after talking to a friend or relative and your doctor. These websites generally offer advice, support, contact information and factual information about a particular illness including symptoms. I know it can be hard to explain yourself and your illness to your loved ones so it's a sensible idea to point them in the direction of these websites. This will help them understand your behaviours better and it will help them recognise any "warning signs". These charities and organisations are based all over the world and a quick search on the internet will take you to the ones that are based in your country. In terms of a distraction, for me at least, they serve as a reminder than I'm not broken, messed up or a bad person. They remind me that my illness is actually more common than I allegedly thought. They remind me that I'm not alone. They remind me that it's ok not to be ok.

73. 7-11 breathing
Breathing techniques are used quite a lot in therapy and emotional management courses. The first therapy group that I ever attended taught me about breathing techniques. I didn't realise how useful they were until I actually tried them. This breathing technique is so simple and effective. I find that this

and other breathing techniques work really well during episodes of anxiety, panic and anger. You can do this whilst on the go but it works best when you're sitting and with your eyes closed so that other things aren't don't get your attention. All you have to do is breathe in, slowly, for seven seconds and then slowly breathe out for eleven seconds, then repeat as many times as you need until you become calm. If eleven is a little too long then you can do nine or ten seconds. The idea of trying to slow and regulate your breathing is to relax your heart rate as it's pumping fast when you're in a state of panic or anger. If you can close your eyes and visualise the numbers in your head when you're counting that will help you carry out this distraction at a steady pace. If this is done correctly you will find that it will calm you down quite quickly. If emotions and thoughts are really intense then ask someone to help count with you. I had a severe panic in a psychiatric ward once and one of the nurses helped calm me down by practising this technique with me. I went from having blurry vision, short breaths and still limbs to being very relaxed in less than ten minutes.

74. Square breathing

This is another breathing technique I learned in group. According to the facilitators this technique is used by the military when under severe trauma. I prefer this technique to the 7-11 as it requires more effort to control yourself, which leads to a state of calm a lot quicker. However if I'm in a severe state I tend to use 7-11 first and then square breathing when I feel like I'm getting back in control. To apply square breathing you must breathe in for three seconds, hold it in for three seconds, breathe out for three seconds and then hold that for three seconds. Then repeat as many times as necessary. When I do this I try to picture a square being drawn with each three second segment. You can push each segment to four or five seconds if you wish. Generally speaking the more intense the panic or anger is the shorter each segment should be. When you start to calm you can increase until you feel much better. Just like 7-11 breathing if you need help applying it that get someone to count with you. I seriously urge you to apply and master this one. I has saved me many times.

75. Remember that the urges will pass

As intense and unpleasant emotions and thoughts can be they do pass. They're not forever. You may have heard this compared to a storm? "The storm will pass" is a common expression used. I can tell you from experience that this is very true and you need to do your best to remember this. This whole book is about doing things instead of giving into your urges and causing destruction or self-destruction. Remembering that the urges will pass sooner or later gives me hope that if I can just hold on for a bit longer and apply one or several of the distractions listed in this book then I can come out the other side of the storm without doing any harm. Remembering that the urges will pass is the very foundation of which all of these other distractions are built upon. During intense episodes I do my very best to remind myself that the urges, and the emotions associated with them, will go away. Sometimes I have to repeat this to myself a few times before applying one or more of the other distractions. It also generally helps when the people around me remind me of this. I find myself reminding other people of this fact as well. If there's one thing from this book that is going to stick with you let it be this technique.

76. Throw a ball to catch

Have you ever seen The Great Escape? During the film the legendary Steve McQueen is sent to an isolated room within the prisoner of war camp where he is being held captive. When he goes to the isolation room, or "The Cooler", he takes his baseball and mitt with him. The idea of this is so he can keep himself occupied with an activity instead of going insane from all the lack of activity and human interaction. Whilst sitting in isolation he throws his baseball across the small room, it bounces off the floor, then off of the adjoining wall and then it flies back into his mitt. If I was stuck I would want to do that instead of letting the isolation get to me. This is a very simple thing to do but the activity of throwing a ball against the floor and wall to catch it makes use of your body and mind, thus making it an effective distraction from unpleasant thoughts. All you need is a bouncy ball, small rubber ones have quiet the ability to bounce, a hard floor and a wall. You can stand or sit. Sitting is easier. Just sit there, throw the ball at an angle so that when it hits the floor it will bounce into the adjoining wall, which should then bounce off of that wall and that's when you need to try and catch it. If you have a ball that isn't bouncy then take it outside, throw it up in the air and try to catch it. You can also do this with another person or in a group, which is what I did in group therapy before. We sat in chairs evenly apart and then threw up to three balls at once, trying to catch them from random throws. Honestly, I found that quite activity very distracting and fun. Keep your eye on the ball.

77. Play a board game

You can probably play against yourself in aboard game but you don't need me to tell you this will be more effective when playing against friends or family. Board games generally take up a lot of thinking power so if you can gather some friends or family to play with then you're in for a treat. I used to have friends round for a board game night, as well as card games, and it was so much fun. It's nice to see people playing and talking with one-another without the use of mobile phones, which is all too common these days unfortunately. The interaction between people whilst playing board games is generally more distracting than the game itself. That is of course if you're not playing something like chess or battle ships, which require more strategic thinking than something like snakes and ladders. There are so many board games, card games and other types of non-video games that you can play with people. I like Cards Against Humanity, Cranium and Trivial Pursuit the most. Board games played with others can be really good fun and/or strategic so either way your mind is going to be highly distracted. Find a couple of games to play, invite some friends over, or play with your family, and just enjoy the moment. If you're more of a competitive person then perhaps chess or Scrabble will distract you more. Whatever you play please put your phone away!

78. Play Jenga

So why have I got Jenga as a separate distraction? First of all you can play this yourself, secondly I learnt to use it as a distraction technique in group therapy and thirdly I believe it takes more concentration than any other game or board game. I didn't realise how distracting Jenga was until we started to play it in group therapy. I could come to group and feel extremely low but a round of Jenga would help lift me into positivity, as long as the game lasted long enough. If you have never heard of Jenga before then all you need to know is that you build a tower out of wooden blocks and then have to remove one block at a time to which you then add to the top of the tower. This must be done over and over again until it falls down. Simple right? It is until you realise that taking one block out might make the entire thing fall over. You can play by yourself but it's better with at least one other person. You can get a small size Jenga for table tops but large ones, which stack over a metre tall, are available too. What I love about Jenga is that it requires a steady hand and forward thinking in order to keep going and this is intensely distracting. If you're competitive like me then your mind will be glued to this game.

79. Close your eyes and listen for sounds

In my group therapy, as a "grounding" exercise, sometimes we would be told to sit, close our eyes and listen out for each individual sound that we could hear. We would hear things like the clock ticking, the birds outside, people walking up and down corridors and doors closing. This distraction is better suited when sitting or laying down. The idea of closing your eyes is so that your hearing sense is more in focus. Try this exercise out quickly now; close your eyes and listen out. What sounds can you hear? Maybe you can put a five or ten minute timer on your phone so you're doing it for long enough. Keep your eyes closed and your body relaxed. The distraction comes from focusing all your attention on all the sounds that are outside of your body. Your hearing sense is now dominating your attention, instead of any unpleasant thoughts and feelings. If there is nothing but silence where you are then perhaps it's a good idea to go outside and sit down when trying to listen to your surroundings. You can do this distraction for as long as you want but around five or ten minutes is effective. When we did this in group we discussed afterwards what we could hear.

If you do this on your own you can write down everything you heard. You might just be surprised how many things you have heard that usually go unnoticed.

80. Pick a colour and look around for things that are that colour

This was another simple "grounding" exercise that we practised in group therapy. At first I found the idea of this to be too simple and that it would have no effect on me. Plus I struggle to identify certain colours due to my colour deficiency. All you have to do is pick a random colour and then start looking around your environment to find things that are that colour. It is simple but it's quite effective. The distraction works because you're constantly trying to find things that match the colour you chose. If you are outside and on the go then you will probably find lots of things that have the colour you chose. If you're practising this in your bedroom, or a place that you spend a lot of time in, you may wish to chose a different colour each time to get the most out of this distraction technique. In group therapy we would do this for five minutes and then share our findings with each other. Also in group therapy the facilitators would pick a colour for all of us to find. If you're with someone then you can pick a colour and get the two of you to find things and see who can find the most.

81. Have a bath or shower

Caring for your body is just as important as it is to care for your mind. Look after your mind and it helps look after your body. It's just as true the other way around; look after your body and it will help look after your mind. Whether you've just woken up or had a busy day it's always good for you to clean yourself in a nice relaxing bath or shower. Personally I prefer to shower as the constant flow of hot running water feels like a massage in some way. Plus the water temperature is consistent. However laying in a warm bath filled with bubbles is very peaceful. There's something about relaxing in the bath or shower that just seems to cleanse my mind as well as my skin. It almost feels like the water is getting rid of my negative thoughts as well as any dirt on my skin. If you prefer baths then why not set a peaceful mood and light some scented candles? It creates a really calm environment for you to enjoy and be at peace with. Perhaps some chill out music in the background too? If you would rather shower instead you could always do what I do. Bring some speakers into the bathroom and turn the music up high and sing along to whatever music you listen to? Please take care of your personal hygiene, it does make a difference to your well-being.

82. Talk to yourself (in the mirror)

I know what you're thinking, "that sounds crazy!" I know it can be a stereotype that only mentally ill people talk to themselves but there's a lot more to it than that. Have you ever noticed that it's easy to give people great advice but it's hard to apply the same advice to yourself? Well, in my studies and research on successful people, and the philosophy of achievement, I have learnt about our inner voice and how it influences us. Stay with me on this. My understanding is that our true inner voice is somewhat of a connection between our minds and the Universe, in other words it's the Universe trying to get a message over to us. This happens more often than we consciously recognise. Ever heard that inner voice when trying to accomplish something? When it tries to encourage you or point you into the right direction? Call it what you wish but that's my understanding of it. That's how I interpret it. Sometimes it's hard to distinguish the difference between messages from the Universe and the inner voice we use to talk to and guide ourselves through conscious thinking. I have experienced both. I have used my inner voice, through conscious thinking, to help guide and motivate myself. I have also experienced messages from the Universe within myself. If you have read my previous book "Self-harm to Self-harmony" you may remember my experience of when I started to turn my life around. But as I said, it's difficult to distinguish the difference between when you're consciously choosing to *think* this inner voice and when it's the Universe communicating with you. Still with me? Well, whether you want to look at it as deeply as I do or not you can use your voice to motivate and guide you. We can give advice to people because we have the mental capacity in our imagination and memory to put together a plan that *should* work. I say "should" because nothing is certain. The problem is that we doubt ourselves, for whatever emotional or psychological reason, and struggle to listen to our own words despite it being perfectly sound or logical advice. If you want to make use of this technique it's best applied when verbally talking to yourself out loud, and better yet, in front of a mirror. I can't begin to tell you how many times I have motivated myself, and guided myself, through talking to myself. Sometimes I speak to myself quite loudly, if no one is around me, and sometimes I whisper to myself. There are times when I talk to myself in my head too. But the point is that I can exercise more control over myself, physically and mentally, when I talk to myself in an assertive way. It's as if my positive and better self, which appears to be wise, is mentoring me into doing the right thing and getting what I want or need. I know this technique seems like a lot to take in but all I suggest you do is talk to yourself out loud about what you want and need, especially need. You can do this in your own head but hearing your own voice through your ears will help motivate you more. Shout at yourself if you have to. The use of a mirror will improve the effectiveness of this technique because you can see yourself talking as if it was another person trying to motivate and guide you. Got a problem that needs solving? Keep asking yourself until the answer comes. Need motivating? Use that voice. Want to make use of your imagination? Tell yourself. Your mind may live with mental illness but I can assure you it's still the most powerful tool in your possession.

83. Make a to-do list and do it

There's more to working through a to-do list than simply getting things done. There's no doubt it's important to keep on top of things in your life and staying active but there's also a biological benefit to ticking things off your to-do list. As you complete each task on your list your brain will release dopamine, which, as you probably know, makes you feel good. But here's how to get the most out of a to-do list. Simply write out a list of things you *need* to do today. Don't write out so many things that you can't achieve them today. Writing out too many things will make it difficult for you to feel motivated enough to do them. Three to five things, depending how much effort is required and how much time you have, is enough for you to feel the benefits of accomplishment. Even completing a to do list as simple as the following example can make you feel better about yourself, as well as distracting you through being active:

1. Make the bed
2. Brush teeth
3. Wash
4. Tidy room
5. Message a friend to see how they are

You can put whatever you want on your list but as I say make sure it's something you can do in a day. The more tasks you don't complete the more likely you will put them on tomorrow's to-do list and you will probably keep doing this to the point of frustration. Procrastination isn't healthy. Another tip is to write the list out on paper and then put it where you can see it. Crossing things off is when the dopamine gets released. Seeing the list in front of you helps keep you on track. You could use a to-do list app on your phone but for some reason, for me at least, it doesn't seem to be as effective at making me feel good. It could be different for you though. If you don't know what to do today then ask someone if they need help with something.

84. Watch bubbles rise in a cup

This is another distraction technique that I learnt through one of my skills groups for people with EUPD/BPD. The facilitators gave us a plastic cup and poured sparkling water into the cup. The idea of it was for everyone to sit comfortably and silently. We were asked to stare into the cup and focus on the bubbles, mostly the bubbles that rose to the surface of the liquid. We were told that the bubbles represented our thoughts and that, like the bubbles, our thoughts will rise to the surface and disappear. Simple yeah? The first time I watched the cup I found myself struggling to focus and my unpleasant thoughts were trying to dominate my mind. However it didn't take long for the bubbles to start holding my attention. The bubbles that stuck to the sides and bottom of the cup did nothing for me, but, the ones that quickly rose to the top did grab my attention. Movement will always have a better chance of holding your attention that something that is completely motionless.

85. Make and use a self-soothe box

This is a popular one. I have not personally made use of this distraction, however, due to the amount of people that have suggested using it I have decided to include it in this book. A self-soothe box is a box that contains items that can help soothe you in times of your emotional episodes. All you need is a box and some things that you can do something with that make you more relaxed or distracted. The idea is that when you feel depressed, anxious, angry, upset, etc. you can go to your box, open it and engage with something from it until your "storm" passes. The box should be filled with multiple items so that you have a choice. One item may work better for you when you're upset, one may work better when your frustrated and one may work better when you're anxious. You can put whatever you want in your box as long as they have a positive influence on your mind, body and emotions. Look around at your belongings. What do you have that makes you smile? What do you have that keeps your hands busy? What do you have that gives you a sense of worth? Here are a list of examples:

- Photos of loved ones
- Cuddly toy
- Photos of happy memories
- Fidget toy
- Favourite book
- Favourite movie
- Favourite album
- Chocolate
- Sketch book and pencil
- Notepad and pen
- Handheld video game console
- Something you bought associated with a happy memory
- A list of phone numbers for phone lines or friends
- A list of your achievements

There's no limit to what you can put in there. Use your imagination. Only you know what makes you feel better.

SUGGESTIONS FROM MY FOLLOWERS

The following distractions are suggestions from my followers on Instagram. I asked them what helps them stay distracted when they're struggling. I have picked the ones I like the most and I have commented on each of them. Thank you to those who took the time to share your distractions. It means so much to me that you care. Your Instagram names are included below.

86. "Run on the spot until I feel my heart pound." - **@ja.ne896**

I've already mentioned about doing exercises to help release endorphins in this book. But running on the spot is something you can do right now or at any given moment. You don't need any equipment and you don't need to go anywhere to do it. It's a quick way to tire yourself out and get an endorphin release. It's also a good way to wake yourself up in the morning!

87. "Running my hands under water… down to my forearms. Cool or hot water both work." - **@lexi_61**

I believe this works in a similar way to using a red pen to draw lines on your arms but on a more "touch" sensory level rather than a "visual" sensory level. I can imagine the water is meant to simulate blood running down your arm that would otherwise come from self-harm. I can also imagine that if you close your eyes whilst doing this it would probably be more helpful as it could help you to imagine the water as blood. Even pinging an elastic band then running the water down your arm with your eyes closed could make it more "real". That may seem a little morbid but we can't shy away from the reality of what can go through the mind of someone who self-harms.

88. "Chew crushed ice." **- @karolinakalinowski**

If you have ever chewed crushed ice, or ice cubes in general, you will know what kind of sensation it brings to your mouth. In fact I just tried this out again to remind myself of what it feels like. Even with just the one ice cube your mouth becomes very cold very quickly. Especially when it starts turning to water. When biting into the ice, keep chewing it until it turns to water instead of swallowing shards of ice. The temperature of the water will send messages to your brain that will get your attention I can assure you. You will probably have to go through several cubes to get the most out of this.

89. "I like to sing because I feel like it's the only way I can express my feelings (or numbness) without cutting or hurting myself in any other way." **- @levitating.goner**

I love this one. I sing a lot in the car. Mostly because it's the only time I can shout and scream to my music when no one is watching. Singing is a very healthy form of expression as well as a distraction. Find the song that fits the mood you're in, or the mood you want to be in, and sing to your hearts content. Singing is like talking but it's more fun.

90. "I just drive around with my best friend. It helps cope with the pain of mental health and being a survivor of rape." **- @georgia_hogan101**

I admire your bravery for sharing this. Driving is a good distraction on it's own, as long as you feel safe enough to get behind the wheel, but having your best friend come along for the journey makes it a lot more safer and therapeutic. If you can't drive but your friend does then being the passenger works well too. I have gone on countless drives with friends to talk about my problems. It's practically a double distraction. Keeping your eyes on the road ahead whist talking to your friend.

91. "Hide under my duvet, snuggled away from anything that can hurt me." **- @rachmm_**

Nothing is quite as comforting as being snuggled up with or under your duvet. Having the duvet wrapped around you gives you a sense of security as well as physical comfort. I have spent many hours under, or hugging, my duvet when feeling miserable. Sometimes it feels like I'm cuddling another person, which helps me feel more at ease. If you end up falling asleep then that's a bonus!

92. "I swim. I used to swim competitively before I got sick but it's still my safe place. The only time I get to think about things is when my head is in that pool." **@elizaas.truth**

Without a doubt swimming is good exercise, and, as you have probably guessed it's going to give you some of those much needed endorphins. I know it can be difficult to want to go swimming if you have scars but you've got to come out of your comfort zone in order to gain more confidence. I personally haven't been for a proper swimming session in years but I know people who get a lot out of it mentally. Just being in the water itself can be very relaxing regards if you want to swim the length of the pool or not.

93. "Play a sensory game like Bop It." **- @wikiigirl**

When I saw this suggestion on my Instagram I couldn't believe I didn't think of this. I used to play this game as a kid and it was very distracting even back then. If you've never played Bop It then give it a go. You have to do what this Bop It device tells you without doing it wrong. It has different parts to the device that you can switch, spin, whack, etc. It's very addictive. Memory games can be really distracting too. Simon Says, the memory game from the 80s I'm referring to, is a great memory game where you have to watch four colours light up in a sequence and then you have to click the colours in the same order. Each round it will add another colour to the sequence making it more difficult. You can look for memory games and sensory games and apps online.

94. "I like to sit in a field, forest or beside water and just relax with nature." **- @mumofnoname**

This is a lovely one. I've always liked the idea of this but have never used it as a distraction. I normally prefer to walk in calm outdoor environments. When I get the opportunity I'm going to give this a go. As you may remember, your environment has a strong influence on your thinking and your behaviour. A calm and peaceful environment can work wonders on you, especially one that has been formed by nature. Rivers, forests, fields, beaches, etc. often look, sound and smell beautiful, which means your thoughts will begin to synchronise accordingly. If you're stuck in a place that feels depressing, claustrophobic, frustrating or anxiety inducing then go outside and find a place in nature that feels harmonious. Sit, relax and take it all in until you begin to feel more at peace with nature and yourself.

95. "Put bracelets on. I always have mine all the way up on my arms so I don't even get to see my own wrists so that my old scars don't trigger me." - **@emopanda_00**

It can be hard for some people to look at their old scars and not think unpleasant things. I'm grateful for the fact that I've gotten past that stage. Having bracelets, wrist bands and other types of accessories to cover them is a great idea, especially during the hotter weather where wearing long sleeve tops isn't an option. During my teenage years I used to wear arm warmers, though I don't see as many people wearing them today. If your old scars do trigger you then cover them in whatever way you can but it would be even more affective to learn to be at peace with them.

96. "Play an instrument or try to learn to play an instrument as creating music can be a great distraction." **- @cema_23**

I miss playing in a band. When I was at the stage of trying fight back against my struggles during my teenage years I invested in a PA system and my friends and I started a band. It didn't last that long but when we practised in my Nan's garage I felt something that I have never felt before. Although I wasn't playing an instrument I still felt alive and proud of myself. I was being creative with lyrics and I was expressing myself. That was one way I got my demons out. I did try to learn guitar as well and I remember how focused I was attempting to learn. Like learning anything that you're passionate about, it was highly distracting. It takes a lot of practice to learn an instrument which means it will take a lot of your attention.

97. "Look at photos that remind you of good things such as days out, etc." **- @carlafarry**

Despite what we believe when we feel low we have had good times in our lives. With today's technology we can capture a moment with our phones, which allows us to look at them in seconds. It's a wise idea to put your favourite photos of happy times into one place so you can remember that life can be good. When we feel negative it's easy to overlook and forget our happy memories so a visual reminder can be invaluable. If you can print out the photos then stick them on your wall where you can see them regularly. If you can't then put them into one folder on your phone, tablet or computer where you can look at them in the time of need. Even if you don't feel low looking at these photos can still re-enforce your positive energy.

98. "I find that getting away and planning any trip helps. Even if it's one night away somewhere for just a change of scenery." - **@surfbabe500**

Going away to some place new or a place that makes you feel good can be very powerful. I've already covered how important the effects of an environment can be on your mind. Going outside for a stroll or sitting down surrounded by nature is powerful but planning a trip or a holiday can be even more powerful. As well as actually going to a new location, or one you have been to before, you can benefit from the anticipation. Planning on going somewhere gives you something to look forward to. Every year I go to the same music festival and I can't begin to tell you how much I look forward to that. It may not be a new place for me to visit but I still get excited all year round. Going there makes me so happy and I never feel negative. It helps me escape and forget my problems. Sometimes we just need a break from reality so we can relax our minds and remember what it feels like to be free. Going away is fairly limitless, as long as you have money of course. Perhaps plan to go away with friends for an event over the weekend? Maybe spend a night in a hotel in a city that you'd like to visit? Why not plan a day at the beach? Or even stay at a B&B in a historical town. The world has places worth visiting and they can all make you forget the shit that you put up with, if only for a day.

99. "Cooking." - **@withdrawlz.b**

Straight to the point here. Cooking is a form of art I can assure you. It requires careful planning and executing. Not to mention great timing. Although that depends on what you're cooking. Food is important for all of us but preparing meals is where the distraction works. You don't need to be amazing at cooking to make it a worthwhile distraction. Outside of my Youth Potential project I'm a chef for a busy hotel. Believe me when I say it's a great distraction. Unlike working in a professional kitchen cooking at home is a lot less stressful. You don't have to worry about people getting pissed off if something goes wrong. If you have cooking skills already then why not go to your local supermarket and get experimental with some ingredients? Make something new. You know that the preparation will

*keep your mind busy right up until the point of eating.
If you have little or no cooking skills then the best
way for you to make use of this distraction is to look
up some recipes, online or in cooking books, and
follow some simple step-by-step instructions that will
help you create a meal that makes your mouth water.
There are plenty of videos online that will teach you
how to cook as well.*

100. "Having someone body check you." -
@selfharmerproblems_

*I have personally not used this technique but I can
easily see how this could work. If you can appoint a
trusted person to check your body on a regular basis
it could be used as an incentive not to hurt yourself.
We don't like to upset people that mean something
to us and them seeing our self-harm can be very
upsetting especially if they are struggling to
empathise with us. Honestly I have never felt good if
my family have seen my cuts but when they did and
expressed a level of care and understanding it did
make me feel relieved and less anxious around them.
If you can get someone to body check you make sure
it's someone who will try to empathise with you. If
you do end up hurting yourself and they see it it's
more likely they will be caring towards you and that's
what you need isn't it? If someone I care about has
asked me if I have cut, and I know they will be
understanding, I feel more inclined to open up to*

them and talk about it. That's the stage you need to be at; opening up to people.

101. "Calm harm app." - **@cevenden13**

Calm harm is a great free app that helps you "ride the waves" of your destructive urges. Once you download the app to your phone or tablet you set your preferences and then can choose from a list of activities. You can choose from the following activities:

- *Comfort*
- *Distract*
- *Express Yourself*
- *Release*
- *Breathe*

You can also choose "Random" and the app will give you an activity at random. Each activity gives you a selection of tasks to carry out that should help you through your urges until they die down. In my opinion they are all forms of distraction techniques, a lot of which you will find in this book, but they are all effective as long as you sincerely try your best. After each activity it will ask you how you're feeling now, whether the urges have passed and a few questions about your urge. Although there are other similar apps available I really like this one as it's very easy to use and has clearly been made with care. Plus it's free.

102. "Geocaching." - @mir_h22

Instead of me writing my comments on Geocaching, as I know very little about it, let Miranda (@mir_h22) share her thoughts and experiences with you:

"For people who don't know what Geocaching is I can really only describe it as a treasure hunt. What you are on the hunt for is something called a Cashe. Cashes can be big or small, they can be out in the open or very well hidden, and sometimes you can search for hours just to find out it was right in front of your face the whole time. If you find a Cashe with items in it you cannot take anything unless you put something in its place even if it's just a penny.

I find Geocaching to be a good distraction for a few different reasons. First I only go Geocaching with my family (husband and daughter) so being with them alone is a good distraction. Geocaching also allows me to get some exercise, which is good for my mental health because it involves walking/hiking in the woods. The last reason Geocaching is such a good distraction is because it's like a treasure hunt and to hunt for that treasure it takes a good amount of mental focus."

Does that sound like something you'd be up for? If so go to www.geocaching.com to find out more.

102 DISTRACTION TECHNIQUES
For Self-harm and other Mental Health struggles

So there you have it. 102 different distractions you can carry out until the urges or "storm" passes. What ones are you going to try next in the time of need? What ones are you going to suggest to a loved one who needs some encouragement? Do you have any that aren't listed in this book?

Despite what you may believe about yourself you are a wonderful person who deserves to be in control of your mental health. You DO have the power to distract yourself from your deepest and darkest thoughts and feelings. But like I said in the beginning of this book, it will take practice and not every distraction works for everyone. For them to work you must try them with *sincerity*. Do not try them half-arsed. Do not try them for the sake of me or anyone else. Try and apply them because *you want them to work*. Try and apply them because you want to be in control. Just because you live with mental illness doesn't mean you're not capable of using that gifted brain of yours. As much as you experience mental illness it doesn't mean your mind is broken or a failed asset. It's always going to be your most powerful asset. It can help you discover new ways of distracting yourself. It can help remind you to distract yourself in the time of need. It can also get you to do constructive things that enable you to care for yourself. And when the time comes when you don't feel strong enough to apply a distraction you MUST turn to someone for help. Communicating to others as a way of distraction, or getting them to help you apply a distraction will never be a sign of weakness. It will always be a sign of strength.

My thoughts on "Recovery"

Recovery is a term that you hear a lot when you experience mental illness. When I was fifteen through till twenty I heard the term brought up a lot in my meetings, appointments and therapy sessions. Before I reached twenty one I truly believed that I had recovered from anxiety and depression. At the time I had not self-harmed for months, I woke up happy each day and everything in my life seemed to fall into place. I fell in love, had two children, had a home, got several promotions and discovered my purpose. I had it all. But in 2017, when my relationship with my partner at the time ended, everything went downhill.

In November 2017 I started to feel depressed and I was cutting myself again. Over the next few months anxiety was also re-surfacing and I tried to take my own life three times. I was diagnosed with emotionally unstable personality disorder, though I was diagnosed with it at the age of nineteen but never realised because I never read the report from the psychiatrist. Ever since my relapse I have been pondering the idea of recovery and my perception of it. I've been asking myself the following questions over and over again:

- What does recovery actually look like?
- How realistic is it to achieve recovery?
- Does the idea of recovery actually help an individual?

The first question is the one I asked the most because I have not been able to give a reasonable or realistic answer. If you look up the word "Recovery" in the dictionary you may find this definition; "A return to a normal state of health, mind or strength". That's what I thought I had achieved at the age of twenty up until my relapse. But after relapsing and learning more about my diagnosis I have started to form a new theory. I believe that recovery is too abstract to conceive and that it can be overwhelming for a lot of people, which is detrimental to your well-being.

Hear me out. Ask yourself, what does recovery look like? Really think about it. Try to picture it. What is your "recovery" vision made up of exactly? Does it mean that you will never feel depressed again? Does it mean you will never feel anxious again? Does it mean you will never think about wanting to commit suicide again? Does it mean your mind will only produce positive thoughts? Does it mean you will always have a smile on your face and that everything will be perfect? I used to think that's what recovery was. I used to try and live my life like that. I tried my hardest to push away every negative thought and emotion that tried to bring me down. I tried to be invincible. I tried to conquer everything that got in my way and I would never give up. Some of my friends and family said I was emotionless. At the time I thought they were wrong, but, upon reflection they were right. What I was doing wasn't healthy.

My thought process was that if I wasn't happy then I must be unhappy, which I didn't want to be. I had to be one thing or another. There was no middle ground. If I wasn't being "recovered" then I was failing. After relapsing I couldn't live that way any more. It was hard to even feel ok, let alone happy. I felt like I had failed and wasted the last seven years of my life. All that hard work of trying to be an indestructible positive force had gone. Why though? I knew what to do to "recover", as I had done it before, but just couldn't do it any more. I couldn't be at peace with myself any more and I felt that I would never be happy again.

At least this time I was wiser so asking for help and medication wasn't a problem. I got back into therapy and started taking my old meds again, thanks to my doctor actually listening to me. Recovery started being thrown around again. I couldn't picture recovery at all and even if I could I didn't feel like it was possible. Every time the mental health professionals spoke to me about recovery it just pissed me off and made me feel worse. "If we could wave a magic wand and make everything bad go away, how would that look?" was thrown at me several times too. I can't wish my feelings away so how the fuck am I supposed to even be in the right mindset to answer something like that? No, trying to achieve recovery is overwhelming and too abstract to even know what it looks like. How are you supposed to achieve something if you can't even explain, define or visualise it? Don't get me wrong, some levels of certain mental illnesses can be overcome. But they are often related to a single events and it also depends on the individual. But in my opinion and experience it's too much for a person to think about recovery. When you feel like your world is falling apart recovery is the last thing on your mind and when people tell you, "recovery is possible", you end up resenting the idea, which makes you a lot worse. And you still can't make a realistic picture of it in your mind.

So what is the answer to living with mental illness? Well, I'm not sure if I have the definitive answer but I have drawn a conclusion that I strongly believe in. I believe in it because it's enabled me to keep on going. My conclusion is this:

"The idea of recovery is too abstract and overwhelming. It's hard to picture. It's a blur that seems like a life time away. I can't wait for recovery and I don't know what to do to even get there. Is there even an end goal for recovery? No, there is not. It's not about recovery. Firstly it's about accepting the fact that you have a mental illness, or are experiencing mental illness. Without this acceptance you will never be able to go forward with the right knowledge. There's no shame in that. Secondly it's about opening up and reaching out. You have to let people know that you need help because they journey ahead is not one you can do alone. There's no shame in that either. Thirdly, learn how to manage your symptoms constructively through distraction and expression. It's an on-going life-long process that has to be regularly practiced. That's why I wrote this book. Finally, remember that when things go wrong it's ok. Through these four principles I have reached a point where I feel balanced enough to enjoy my life again and keep going. Sometimes I can distract myself, sometimes I can't. Sometimes I feel happy, sometimes I don't. Sometimes I experience the symptoms of my illness, sometimes I don't. Sometimes I need help, sometimes I don't. Sometimes I feel like I can achieve things, sometimes I can't. Sometimes I can talk to people about my feelings, sometimes I can't. There is no right or wrong in this. It's just being human. My illnesses will always be with me and I'm cool with that. But I will never aim for recovery. I'm not putting that kind of

pressure on myself. Honestly, I'm happy living this way. I don't feel like I've failed if I cut myself. I don't feel like a fake if I'm happy for the day. I don't feel under pressure to be a certain way. For me, this is a way of life that I can accept and go forward with."

Thank you.

Printed in Great Britain
by Amazon

66625408R00059